LANDSCAPE WITH SMALL HUMANS

John Whitworth

by the same poet
*

Tennis and Sex and Death

Drawing of John Whitworth (aged 47) by his daughter Eleanor (aged 9), 1993.

Landscape With Small Humans

JOHN WHITWORTH

PETERLOO POETS

First published in 1993
by Peterloo Poets
2 Kelly Gardens, Calstock, Cornwall PL18 9SA, U.K.

© 1993 by John Whitworth

**A CIP catalogue record for this book is available from
the British Library**

ISBN 1–871471–40–0

Printed in Great Britain by
Latimer Trend & Company Ltd, Plymouth.

821.914
25.033

ACKNOWLEDGEMENTS are due to the editors of the following journals and magazines in whose pages some of these poems first appeared: *The Spectator, London Magazine, The New Statesman, The Independent, Honest Ulsterman, Poetry Book Society Anthologies 1* and *3*.

Supported by

CORNWALL
COUNTY COUNCIL

LIBRARIES AND ARTS

INVESTMENT
SOUTH WEST ARTS

BIOGRAPHICAL NOTE

I wasn't born in England. I was born in India—Nasik, near Bombay, now a large industrial town. But emotionally that's just rumour backed up by certain artefacts and some old friends of my father's.

Hatch End is a North London suburb on the Bakerloo Line between Harrow and Watford—'Hatch End For Pinner' the boards at the railway station said. Pinner is Metroland of course, but I had always thought, and indeed rather hoped, Hatch End was entirely without historical-biographical distinction except such as Whitworth the Poet would graciously confer. But that is not so, for it is the birthplace of Mrs Beeton and also, delightfully, the home of *Poet and Printer*, the poetry publisher.

Just before and after the First War, Hatch End grew up as a superior commuter suburb. The houses in The Avenue, the long road where we lived, were big ones, and all different, as if put up severally over a period rather than all at once by a builder. I remember being happy there and perhaps I really was.

The move to Edinburgh was in 1955 and so upsetting that for years I retreated into the woods and fields of my Lost Domain, principally through the works of Richmal Crompton (I was Ginger). But I suppose some other defence against puberty would have arisen if the family had stayed where they were. Poems maybe.

As well as being about all that, the text seems, rather neatly, to be about The Fifties, so comfortably different, and, as I can see now the poems are all together, about my mother who died in January 1961.

The three schools are, in Hatch End, Grimsdyke Primary, and in Edinburgh, James Gillespie's Boys, a mile distant from the Girls, celebrated by Muriel Spark as The Marcia Blaine School, and the old Royal High, now as empty as the Doric temples it so much resembles.

Contents

page

ENGLAND

SCOTLAND

ENGLAND

Joffy and Me

Over the railway bridge we found the stream
With a tractor tyre, pram wheels and odds and ends.
I bagged the bits to make a go-cart from
While Jonathan heaved the tyre out, two best friends.
Since kindergarten it had been the same,

Being so unalike, living so near:
Joffy was lowering, dark, a stammerer
Top-notch at games, where I was fair and bright,
Scouring fresh libraries for books to gut,
Last to be picked at football and all that.

We stood a-tiptoe on the bridge and touched
The humming wires that looped from pole to pole,
Or, to be accurate, he did. I watched,
Leary of megavolts, till he grinned unscathed
And swung me up beside him on the wall.

Up there you could see for miles, across the mess
Of roofs and streets and gardens, to the blue
Horizon over Northwood. Happiness
Was no more than a habit then. We knew
You could have it always, if you wanted to.

Here Is My Space

34, The Avenue, Hatch End,
Middlesex. I liked to keep it neat,
Commas and capitals for our House, our Street,
Our Village. Then our County, obsolete
Since the L.C.C. of Herbert Morrison.

Yet London was not us—you took a train,
The steam maroon or the electric brown,
To Queen's Park, then the little red one down
The nasty, echoing hole, and London Town
Was dark above us in its fog and rain.

It had the new Queen, sitting on a horse,
The Oval, Madame Two-Swords, Gamages
(A toyshop where we queued for bloody ages),
The great black river jostling with barges
And all the famous buildings on the sauce.

These were somewhere else. The great good place was ours:
Our railway bridge, our stream, our library,
Our bus to Pinner and the ABC
For our Saturday Morning Pictures. Why should we
Want more or different? This was how it was.

Fictions

Tell about India, she said to me,
When you were a little boy.
                I said I slept
On a verandah, like a balcony,
Until, into my cot one night, there crept
A dark and dangerous thing. What could it be?

It could have been a crocodile, she said.
Or some nocturnal beast (it being night)
Or a huge, poisonous snake. Snakes in your bed?
Yuk! Or a prowling tiger, come to bite
Your bottom (*Tee-hee!*), come to kill you dead.

It was a leopard, and it crept away
Back to the jungle, I said.
                I'm not clear
How wild the country is around Bombay.
I suppose there could have been some jungle near
In 1946. But I don't say

My father shot it from his bedroom door.
The cub the darkness made a baby-killer
Became the skin my pirate sister wore
On the big lawn behind our big white villa
In Middlesex in 1954.

The Long Divorce

My father's hurrying to The Board of Trade
Down New Elizabethan colonnades.
Sycamores weep their still-imperial map
Of leaves, and fat Churchillian conkers drop;
Dad squelches down; The milkman's horse clops up.

Could it have been just seven years ago
They snapped the sahib outside his bungalow—
A thirty-three-year-old magnifico
Who governed India from horses' backs,
Collector (that's collector of the tax)?

And the memsahib crisp and smiling at his side,
His childhood sweetheart and his year-long bride
(She had a horse as well, and she could ride),
With, cuddled to his *ayah*, by her knee,
One little Whitworth Empire made—that's me.

Three scrambling, cockney Whitworths now of course,
Our imperial echoes down to HP sauce,
Our servant problem shrunk to Mrs S.
Who *does*, the patrician memsahib busy Bess,
Our Mummy in her Marks & Spencer's dress,

And just the milkman's and the coalman's horse.

Primary Colours

I shared a desk with Gillian. She could wink a
Lovely blue eye, and when I read *Old Lob*
She touched my hand, which made my ears go pinker
Like Piglet's. Duncan Saggers did Big Jobs
Again, right there in his pants, the little stinker.

Please Miss, that Duncan Saggers's gone and done
His business.
      Pig face, I never.
             But he had.
And what could you expect? We carried on
With Old Lob's farmyard, Mrs Hen and bad
Black Percy Chick, her errant favourite son.

A bad, black child inside a good, pink Britain
Inside a good and pinkish world, much bigger
Then—*Beano* missionaries were boiled and eaten
And Marks & Spencer sweaters came in nigger
Brown and black cricket teams were always beaten.

We burgeoned on an earth without surprise —
It'd seen both Japs and Jerries off the year
I entered it. How should we recognise
As ours (it was not ours) the pain and fear
In Stinky Saggers' brimming Bambi eyes.

Neighbours

Ours was the semi with bohemian neighbours.
He was an actor on the radio,
Mrs Dale's Diaries and Children's Hours.
Now he does butlers and solicitors
In ads and serials. It's a face you know,

Ascetic, vulturine, an unbritish face.
His wife, the real unbritish, from Vienna,
Spoke German to their pert, precocious daughter
And made strange stews with yoghourt and paprika,
Which was exotic for the time and place.

In England, then and now, such difference matters.
While she went out to work, he loafed all day
Fixing the car, and lobbing googlies at us.
He took us to The Oval where I sat as
Happy as Larry, watching Peter May.

He barracked Barrington's hard-working duck.
He backed into a Bentley, and said, 'Fuck!'
Three more things other grown-ups didn't do.
The pert, precocious, only daughter grew
Up beautiful, but not for me, worse luck.

Non-U Turns

We didn't have a television, which
Was quite acceptable, or even clever,
Though two doors down they had one, being rich.
He was in Cocoa Futures or whatever;
I can't suppose I knew. She was a bitch,

According to some over-sherried grown-up
Oblivious of little pitchers' ears.
There was a deal of arms and eyeballs thrown up,
Slammed doors and yelling *Bloody Hell!* and tears.
Children ought not to see their betters shown up,

So Saturdays and holidays between
The hours of five and six she kept the lid on,
Splutterings and cracklings prologue to a scene
Damped down because we had *The Cisco Kid* on.
We sat cross-legged before the flickering screen,

Holding a chocolate biscuit or a glass
Of orange juice with their posh-blazered sons
Who swore. One of them said he'd show his arse
Reciprocally to my sister once
But she turned him down.
          The vagaries of class.

Gracious Living—Late Georgian

On Monday mornings things were pretty fraught:
Mummy and Mrs Sole would have to sort
Clothes for the washing copper (blue enamel
On three bow legs, as awkward as a camel).
It all took longer than you might have thought.

You boiled the sheets and towels in Family Tide,
Then mangled them, one person to each side,
Then pegged and propped them. When it rained you whipped
Them up onto the pulley where they dripped
On unsuspecting heads until they dried.

There was the washboard and the sink of course
And big green Fairy Soap and the clothes horse
For different stuff, for 'delicates' I think.
Anyway, you had to do them in the sink.
There was steam, and scummy water on the floors.

There was late elevenses where Mrs Sole and
Mummy (who'd given up) shared Woodbines. 'Stolen
Pleasures!' Mummy winked complicity;
I dunked my biscuit in her Ricory;
Let's leave the Fifties at a semi-colon;

Though there's coloureds that you mustn't boil to do,
Damping and Ironing, Starch and Bleach and Blue …

Porridge and Syrup

Mummy made porridge when the winter came,
And soaked left-over crusts to give the birds.
With Golden Syrup you could write your name,
Letting it drop in slow, translucent curds.
I didn't much like porridge all the same

And dawdled. Cormorant brother ladled scoff in
To win five minutes with the electric Hornby.
I watched my cursive J, O, H, N soften,
Wondering could the point of being born be
School and then Work. I thought about it often.

Five days a week, and Saturday mornings too,
Off to the Office (that's what Daddies do):
Coffee and toast and Oxford marmalade
For a Civil Servant at The Board of Trade,
Then the Brown Electric or the Bakerloo

To a horrid place like school you've got to go to,
But a lot worse than school—it lasts so long:
For years and years, till you fill up your quota,
Till the batteries fade on your electric motor
And you settle down to cribbage or mah-jong.

The New Elizabethans

You could trawl for junk where watercress had spread
In the shadow of a willow's overhang,
But not that day. We were hurrying home instead
With awful news, and breathy trebles sang
On kitchen doorsteps. *Mummy, the King's dead.*

Lung cancer at 52. They all smoked then,
Bogart, the King and Mummy. With her hat
And her handbag, Woodbines, in their pale green ten,
Stood on the dresser. Full Strength Navy Cut
For him, I suppose, being a naval man.

The King's dead, Mummy. I'd got my oar in first.
This was a fresh experience, this dying,
This human dying, though our cat got squashed.
Sun flecked the parqueted hall. Mummy was crying.
Little brother bit his lip. I was nonplussed.

Did we KNOW him then? *He never wanted it.*
You do your duty, John. Her proper poise
Restored, specs stuck back on, the cigarette
Relumed, there was toast and Marmite for her boys,
The baby to be bathed, dinner to get.

Haircut

While Mummy trails the push-chair round the queues
I watch a fat man shaved inside the shop.
The razor gleams; it's like the gangsters use.
The barber hones it on his leather strop
With a swishing sound. My dad's got one of those;

I'm seven soon, but he still won't let me try.
I'm reading *Picture Post* and the old King
Stares from the front. His death made Mummy cry
And he looks as sad and sick as anything,
Like my Uncle Douglas did, who didn't die.

It's hot. My legs are sticking to the chair.
Perhaps he took *Brand's Essence, Tonic Yeast*
Or *Phyllosan*—so now his 'outlook's fair'.
My little brother, combed and brushed and greased,
Is clambering down in drifts of butchered hair.

'Short back and sides, young sir?' The barber's keen.
He nicks my ear. Blood bubbles. I am brave.
Wilkinson, Zam-Buk, Durex, Brilliantine.
The fat man rises, gleaming, from his shave
And the old King sleeps for ever in his grave.

Medicinal

DETTOL's got a super hospital-y smell,
But the really serious stuff is IODINE,
Horrid, poisonous purple-staining, hurts like hell.
It's the bleeding and the hurting keep you clean
While it's killing all the germs to make you well.

Cuts can be titchy. *Wounds* are always vast.
So there's different sizes of ELASTOPLAST
Which is lovely. You can pick at it for ever
Till it floats up in the bath. That's if you're clever
And you don't let grown-ups rip it off too fast.

If you're *bunged-up* with an awful tummy-ache,
SYRUP OF FIGS is what you have to take.
Stuffed-up nose (not bum)? It's generally best
To inhale FRIARS' BALSAM. That's while you're awake.
Then at bedtime Mum rubs VICK onto your chest.

Then there's bags more stuff to *keep you regular.*
EX-LAX, ENO'S, ANDREW'S, MILK OF MAGNESIA.
Got the trots? CREAMOLA JUNKET's what you eat.
ZAM-BUK OINTMENT soothes your Granny's aching feet.
COD LIVER OIL sets kiddies up a treat.

There's a jar, a tube, a bottle or a tin
For a thousand ills. And then there's ASPIRIN.

Brave New World

Craig was my first American. He had
A shirt checked like a tablecloth, and hair
Whose shade and bristly feel was like the pair
Of clothes-brushes presented to my dad
In British India when we were there.

Craig knew how sex worked and he told us fanny,
Which we supposed … you know, was only bum.
He was boastful (Yanks were like that, said my granny,
Who had a battery of apothegm)
And I think he thought all British kids were dumb,

But what the hell? He lent out Superman,
Batman and Captain Marvel, and for tough,
Sophisticated guys, maturer stuff
From The Big Country—HORROR COMICS, rough
In execution, rougher still in plan:

The hump-backed ravishing dwarf, the murderess grilling,
Tonsured and wired in Sparky's iron fist,
The lonely sailor lured to serial killing
By the saucer-eyed, sex-deviant hypnotist,
The crabs from Mars, the werewolf from the mist …

Whoever dreamed such wonders could exist?

The Sun and Stars are Mine

Like a little gargoyle perched on a greasy girder,
With shoes hooked round in a way that gives prehensile
Strength to the knees and can feel like bloody murder,
I mark my lesson with a stub of pencil
In The Book Of Numbers. What could be absurder?

Hey ho the wind and the rain and the bare bits chapped —
The shirt-tails out and the windcheater outgrown,
The heavy-armour shorts that won't adapt
To a bum but keep a profile of their own,
The home-knit socks half-mast where the garters snapped.

There's your wild-life stuff when it's *Out With Romany*
On Hill And Moor but that isn't so terrific.
Barn owls and questing voles are hard to see,
Unlike a *Stanier Duchess Class Pacific*.
Anyway, I prefer machinery,

And steam machinery beats all the rest:
The brass-bound *Granges, Manors, Castles, Kings,*
On our seaside summer holidays out West;
Christmas in Edinburgh means, above all things
Gresley A4s —non-stop, streamlined, just the best.

The Snares of Art

The path to the Sunday School was dark. You could
Get to the bend by walking backwards, then
Put in some serious praying. Save me, Lord,
Save me from trolls and kidnappers. Amen.
Make haste to where the Guardians of the Word

Palaver weekly on the poor and needy,
And how The Christian Life is common-sense:
Fair wisps of girls in jerkins, talc-and-tweedy
Spinsters with bosoms, hairy-nostrilled gents
Whose suited bums and elbows shine. How seedy

Do Jesus' massed battalions appear
Beside the suave ungodly, coruscant
With pleasurable sin. It isn't fair.
Is goodness never getting what you want
And withering on the stalk until the clear

Himalayas of Heaven on a cloud?
I licked my pallid Sunday pencils (paints
That spread unholy mess were not allowed),
Marshalling my doubtful squad of popish saints,
Polychromatic, iridescent, proud.

Never Had It So Good

His Stellar-Cruiser soars like a cathedral.
In silver spectacles the god descends.
Children are scattering garlands where he stands
Robed with technology, and his two hands
Upraise in one ebullient dihedral.

Now *We Like Ike:* outside our Hatch End home
See Uncle Harvey's pink, two-hundred horse
Convertible—a Thunderbird of course.
Its radiator teeth are stopped with chrome:
They flash debauch and dollars and divorce,

Hollywood, San Francisco, New Orleans,
Manhattan, Sunset Strip, Miami Beach,
Jive, jazz-band, juke-box, jitterbugging, jeans ...
Not rationing, sago pudding and spring greens,
Not Billy Cotton, Burberries and bleach.

A water pistol like a tommy gun,
A helicopter that WILL REALLY FLY,
A walkin', talkin', livin' doll. *Have fun!*
We'll drive out in the T-bird by and by,
Eh kids? The post-war boom has just begun.

Our purse-lipped parents think it's overdone.

Daggers of the Mind

Snuggle down, John. The night-light flickers palely.
I've scrubbed my teeth and gabbled through my prayers.
Up on the wall the face of Trevor Bailey
Is something devilish, hollow-eyed and scaly
And Mummy's step grows fainter down the stairs.

I've checked for robbers underneath the bed.
No robbers—lots of string, a tin of paint,
My snack of salad cream on sandwich spread
On pickled beetroot on well-buttered bread,
And a half-crown paperback— *Call For The Saint.*

So *Simon Templar turned into the alley*
And was instantly alone. Downtown Chicago
And AN AMMONIA GUN. Crumbs—it's Death Valley
Down there. But The Saint's O.K. He doesn't dally—
The fastest thing since Wells met up with Fargo.

The pages turn themselves. The torch grows dim.
The night-light smokes and starts to deliquesce.
Big Barrelhouse Bilinski's looking grim.
A right cross to the jaw should do for him—
POW! And The Saint obliges with noblesse.

Home Entertainments

We knew a pale and bony girl called Coral,
About twelve maybe (she seemed grown-up to us),
Who interrupted our Meccano quarrel
And the everlasting Test match on the grass,
With games that were strict, imaginative and moral,

Taking in both the vivacity of crime
And the satisfactoriness of punishment.
It worked like this: in a well-drilled pantomime
I crashed the blunt and bloodstained instrument
Onto my brother's bonce time after time,

Eviscerating with a kitchen knife
His nearly breathless corpse. Or he might be,
In Mummy's nightie and high heels, the wife
Drowned in the water-butt. Then the murderer (me),
Quaking with fear, stood trial for his life.

Coral, in some great-aunt's big, black-veiled hat,
Did judge and executioner. The rope
Was knotted on, a prayer said, then SPLAT!
Justice triumphant. These days, where's the scope,
With videos and such, for games like that?

Wheels

Daddy hasn't got a car. We have to walk.
Sunbeam Talbot, Singer Hunter, Humber Hawk,
Jaguar, Jowett, Jensen, Bristol, Frazer-Nash,
When I ask he says we haven't got the cash
Which isn't true, just silly grown-ups' talk.

Joffy's got one (are they richer than us then?).
Triumph Mayflower, Standard Vanguard, Standard 10,
Hillman Minx, Lagonda, Zephyr Zodiac,
And they sit on bits of carpet in the back
Just like the plumber's or the painter's men.

There's a bloke next door who hasn't got a bean,
Rolls Royce Silver Wraith Grand Touring Limousine,
Armstrong Siddeley Sapphire, Bentley Continental,
But he's buying 'Sally' on a sort of rental;
He knows she's more than simply a machine.

No, it's not like aeroplanes or caviare.
Morris Oxford, Morris Minor Traveller,
Vauxhall Cresta, Vauxhall Velox, Vauxhall Wyvern,
In the USA the cinemas are drive-in.
In the Fifties *everybody's* got a car.

What about a little one to make a start in?
M.G. Midget, Austin Healey, Aston Martin.

Wish You Were Here

For two whole weeks our family went away
To the seaside for a Summer Holiday.
Swelling with sulks and temper, everyone
Subsided on the train from Paddington
And settled grimly down to having fun:

At Weston-Super-Mare, a paying guest,
I heard no news of Compton in the Test;
Somebody's golden sands left a deposit
On towels and bathing-things; at Paignton (was it?),
The lavatory was a Sanfect closet,

A chemical and crumbled earth affair,
Whose toilet roll was *Sporting Life* cut square —
I had ten days of constipation there;
And the Dorset dog's dead, deliquescing torso,
Daily observed definitively more so.

Yet once there was a tented county match
Where Godfrey Evans took a stunning catch,
And once, in wellies, splashing through a patch
Of dappled stream, we stopped till, very near
We saw an otter's glistening head appear.

Do you know, I can't remember where we were?

General Election 1955

Dad, there's a girl at school whose dad votes Labour,
A dumpy girl called, dumpily, Joan Stubbs.
It was Morrison, our not quite next-door neighbour,
A seconder in the same cubs
As me, who was hellish hot at giving snubs

And a man to know, except I partly thought
I didn't like him, Christopher Morrison said.
And she did not deny it (I'd drop dead
Before I gave a handle of that sort).
Dad, are we Conservatives? Dad shook his head

And lowered his *Manchester Guardian.*
My heart sank with it. Mr Churchill won
The War. Mr Churchill beat Hitler.
Could we be Socialists like that Stubbs creature
(Christopher Morrison's phrase) when everyone

Was a Conservative at Grimsdyke School?
I think I'll probably vote Liberal,
Said my father, returning to his paper,
And Mum?
   Your mother's not political.
Why do you ask?
     Nothing, dad.
       And just as well
I'd kept it dark that our proper next-door neighbour,
The actor chap, he actually *was* Labour.

Interesting Times

Pan Paperbacks supplied the reading matter:
Boldness Be My Friend, The Wooden Horse,
Enemy Coast Ahead by Wing-Commander
Guy Gibson V.C. D.S.O. D.F.C. and bar,
The Colditz Story, I read them all of course.

I knew a Spitfire from a Hurricane,
A Wellington's extraordinary design,
The layout of a pocket battleship,
That Rommel was a decent sort of chap
And the Gestapo planned to do him in.

At the pictures, Michael Redgrave, Kenneth More,
Pipe-smoking Richard Todd and Leo Genn
Were British Officers and Gentlemen
And demonstrated how we won the War
With understatement and esprit-de-corps.

Though I brilliantined my haircut, brushed my teeth,
Swallowed my Virol, drank my Ovaltine,
Time squandered my appointment with the Hun.

So must the Britons, with the Romans gone,
Have huddled in their smoky huts beneath
Mysterious monuments of striding stone.

Blood and Sand

Because we're still too poor to get a car
Mummy sends us to The Pictures on the bus.
When the driver gets to Pinner cinema
We ping the thingy so he stops for us.
One time he didn't, and a hellish fuss

The huge and horrible conductor made!
We've got a *Workers Playtime* jokey one
Who's 'good with children'—viz. a fusillade
Of Cockney patter like a scatter gun
To make me drop my money. *Blimey son,*

Does yer MUVVER know yer out? Why don't I say
Lor lumme luvaduck mate? Privilege,
That siphons stalactites of snot away,
Squats on my tongue, as every Saturday
The Paleface braves the Pass and, on the ridge

Apaches of the prefabs, roarers, swearers,
All sprawl, brawl, cat-call, tall, torn jersey wearers
Crêpe-soles-on-the-seat-in-front, wild Woodbine sharers,
Rude pictures handed round like contraband,
Bad Language, Sex and Violence, Blood and Sand.

(The films are U certificate and bland.)

Small Samaritan

Walking from cubs back up The Avenue
I saw suns on the pavement, dark red suns,
Shining like blood. I smudged an idle shoe
Across this constellation, and at once ...
Like blood? A line of bloody splashes to

The kerb, a bigger splash and then they crossed.
Panic erupted. Grown-ups had the maps
For territory like this, and I was lost.
But Baden-Powell says when you find a corpse
DON'T PANIC. Right. No body. Nothing. Just

An old lady in a hat, respectably
Done out, straight back, dark handbag. So it's all
All right. Yes it *is*. But no it wasn't. She
Collapsed so fast onto a garden wall
Silk knickers flashed. The cub squeaked, *Pardon me,*

D'you ... ? and the wild old lady dabbed her head
With a little, lace-edged handkerchief. *I fell.*
Old people do. It's my own house I need
Right here. Go home, child. I shall do very well.
DYB DYB. DOB DOB. She bared her teeth and bled.

Later I thought: does it count as my good deed?

New Navigators Circumcise the Globe

The air-raid shelter smelt of turpentine
And rain and cooking-apples. My friend Joffy
Had shown me his so I had to show him mine.
There was all that stuff I couldn't do for toffee —
Overarm serving, playing down the line ...

And now some more. Did I know I couldn't SCREW?
Honest Injun, Cross My Throat and No Duff Gen.
Well, I'd read more books than stupid Joffs. I knew
I was the same as millions of men —
Every Mohammedan and every Jew

And Jesus who was perfect, which should clinch
Things, surely? Surely. All the same, I'd rather,
Through the howling deserts of the sexual pinch,
Be Joffy, or my brother, or my father,
Armed with that extra Gentile quarter inch,

The drachm to tilt the balance from not quite,
Than me, unwhole, unwholesome, pricked to be
A scholar-mendicant, a cenobite,
An Artist. When I asked Mummy, she
Said it was hygiene.
                    That could *not* be right.

Just William

The Secret Chronicles Of William Brown:
Violet Elizabeth microwaves the cat.
A legless Botty staggers back from Town,
Gooses Miss Milton at the Laundromat,
Then pisses into Lady Markham's hat.

With Mars Bars, Jumble and a pint of stout
Ethel astounds the Hadley Tennis Dance
Till Hubert's Skinheads put her up the spout.
Robert, who's into silicone, comes out
Like Dolly Parton. Mother finds Romance

With the Soul Sisters squatting at the Hall,
And, from a teepee in the South of France,
She faxes back a note. *I've done with aunts*
And darning socks and washing underpants.
Stuff that!. Stuff what? Her husband stuffs it all.

He writes (it nets a million in The States)
A bodice-ripper *(SPURNED!)* by dictaphone;
At the Old Barn, The Outlaws, puffing Weights,
Inflating Ginger's Durex, swilling crates
Of Mild, play strip pontoon with Vi and Joan.

You thex-thtarved bathtardth, you can have my dreth,
Daft thods! says Violet Elizabeth.

SCOTLAND

The Scottish Chiefs

Scotland the Brave—The Wallace and The Bruce,
Those stubbly toughs with Caledonian calves,
McEwans Heavy makes their jungle juice.
Ten pints (they don't do anything by halves)—
Their long moustaches bristle as they sluice

Straight glasses of it down with whisky chasers.
Can ye get a whisky in the top o' this,
Eh pal? Ye can? Then fill it up. Ungracious
Speech is their savage art, the Paisley Kiss
That staves your face in, their erotic basis.

This gringo got an expert at the lingo,
But stayed a prancing softie underneath,
As pink and fluttery as a flamingo,
As frangible before the clash of teeth
As kites garrotted when you let the string go.

They did for Wullie though. They fetched the *polis*
Who stitched him up, then battered him apart.
His blackened limbs hung up like broken brollies
Flapped in the wind. Big Rab fair broke his heart.
So sad, so long ago. Poor Bruce. Poor Wallace.

Too Clever By Half

One thing I learned (and there is lots and lots,
Some good, some bad, and some just different,
A nine-year-old *can* learn about the Scots):
Unlike the average Southern prole or gent
They have an honourable place for swots.

But scratch most Englishmen and you will find
A levelling, lethargic state of mind,
Stupidity and snobbery combined.
To them the very thought of thought is bad
And poets and philosophers are mad.

Those Edinburgh Scots were hard and glacial.
They called me shitface but the thing was racial,
And with my origins, not my cleverness
The problem lay. I did, with some success
Slough off *some* unappealing Englishness:

I cannot love a lumpen, grovelling fool;
I cannot love a swine picked out to rule
Because his father paid a boarding school
To polish up his vowels and learn sod-all
Except to swing a bat and kick a ball.

Egotist-fascist-puritanical:
I am a Scotsman in my very soul.

Culture Shock

Our Scottish house was grey and vertical.
It didn't have a fence; it had a wall
Too high to climb, and nothing was the same.
At school they called you by your second name;
In working hours I wasn't John at all.

My teacher was the knobbly sort of Scot
Who cracks his chalky knuckles. He had got
The voice of Moloch or Beelzebub —
GRUBBY — His name was Mr Wilfred Grubb;
Some might have smiled at that, but I did not.

Big school-bags banged big Edinburgh legs,
Foul language skirled like Highland philabegs:
SHEEP-SHAGGER, WANKER, POOF, BUM-BANDIT, TWAT,
FL, VD and FTP (*what's that?*).
The whole first term I tiptoed round on eggs:

The boys were gaunt and cruel like Indian braves.
They piled their hair in Tony Curtis waves.
One wore sharp chisel toes, played mean guitar
And pissed his insolent parabola
Through the lavvy window, singing JESUS SAVES.

Soft-spoken, soft of soul, a pulpy mess,
I scorned my caterpillar Englishness.

New House—New Bearings

Proprieties invested Greenhill Place.
It was Edinburgh South, a carapace
Of Marchmont, Morningside, the Grange, the Manse
And full-strength Capstan in the wooden trams
That took us Wednesdays over to my Gran's

Where Crawford's cakes and doilies fortified
Her moated Grange against the Causewayside:
Small, muttering men, wives wheeling junk-filled prams
Past eyeless tenements and dark back greens
Where babies bawled and boys had spewed their load:

Fierce, godless people who were not our people.
Yet churches climbed to Christ like runner beans:
United Reform, Reform, United Free,
Free, Baptist, Anabaptist, Methody,
Our Pisky Palace with the tallest steeple,

All holiness (except the Catholic sort)
At Holy Corner where they had no pubs,
Just good flats like my other Granny's flat,
Good shops, banks, dentists, where I went to cubs,
And a lampless entry about halfway from school.

A bad man there had made me hold his tool.
It jumped and he giggled when I told him that.

New Boy

Tall school in an old part of town,
Straight from *The Beano*, the old headmaster's gown,
And the close smell of dark desks bound with iron.
Only the words are new: this is a JOTTER,
And the stranger next to me, that boy's my NEIGHBOUR.

I fear my teacher, Mr Grubb, because
I know his tall, dark desk contains a TAWSE
Of iron-black leather, to preserve The Laws,
(God's and The Examiners'), a holy terror
Against persistent idleness and error.

Though Mr Grubb is stern in a tall, bow-wow
Style, he is also kind and roused but seldom
To strike small boys. In this he is unlike some:
Across the passage one demented cow
Batters the living daylights out of them.

Tall tales of blood and of bones that break,
Of a lash across the face for giving cheek,
Dark tales keep a nine-year-old awake:
Why have they brought me to this barren land,
Frantic with vowels I cannot understand,
Where the devils mark their souls into my hand?

A Language Lesson

I used to sit with Colin, my fat friend,
Backs to the wall and bums well off the pitch,
(Your immigrant is well advised to blend)
Mad *fitba'* raged before us, end to end
From blazered railings down to the *kludgie*, which

Is Scots for lavatory, as I called ours
Where I studied English County Cricket scores
In tame defiance. Scottish Colin's fat
Was existential—he ate Bounty Bars
While catechizing me on this and that.

Going the messages means shopping, *roan*
Means drainpipe, rolls are *baps*, and alley's *vennel*.
Your Scot'll never tease. He *takes a loan*
O' donnert folk—whit sort o' folk, ye ken, 'll
Be toffee-nosed (with accents like my own).

I hammered at it nightly in my prayers:
Please God, make me pure Scots in word and deed.
And God is good. Now, if I cross the Tweed,
I feel the blood within me rise, *Here's tae us*
Wha's like us? Bluidy few, an' they're a' deid.

(Via Birmingham it happens at Carstairs.)

Having the Nose for It

The taste of blood's medicinal teaspoonfuls
Slow trickling down your throat was sweet and warm,
And it meant three-quarters of an hour off school,
Flat on the floor of an echoing classroom.
As I lay unmoving, bare legs to the cool

Linoleum, and eyes screwed shut, I tried
To summon solitude and silence; if
You concentrated, all the airy, wide
Contingencies of life beyond the cliffs
Of scarf and burberry on either side,

Milk-bottle clunks, loud whispers, giggles and
Occasional crumps of anger, simplified
Themselves into a tapestry of sound
Like the swish of leaves and birdsong. Then you died,
Then you caught your fluttering soul in your cupped hand

And loosed it down a dust-filled shaft of sun —
The poet habit, hammered from defeats.
So the four-eyed twats, unhandy with a gun,
Drowsing deliciously, could feel like Keats
And, had I heard of him, I would have done.

Byron Lied About His Batting

Like Churchill's pudding, life must have its theme:
When Mr Grubb our teacher, who was strict
But fairly fair, announced that I was picked,
Scorer and Twelfth Man in Fat Colin's team,
It changed my life. My life became a dream,

A dream of flashing drives that take me towards
My undefeated century at Lords,
Of Aussies routed with my double hat-trick —
The hushed crowd gapes and gasps and, awed, applauds
The new master of the ball-trick and the bat-trick?

Well no! I must be truthful: at the wicket
On Fortune's cap I was not the very button,
The pitch was not a stage for me to strut on
And I had no thoughts of being a second Hutton.
This was real. This was earnest. This was cricket.

And yet my life did change. I did forswear
The mad genius with electric hair
That I had been. I was a cricketer
And to be young was (sometimes) very heaven
In Colin's Second Junior XI.

Swimming Lessons

Jimmy Buchanan was an average boy
The awkward sort a clever teacher's pet
Like me would find it easy to forget,
Except as knees and ears and elbows — yet
I do remember him. I'll tell you why:

Old Scobie was the athlete run to fat
Who taught boys of eleven how to swim
(Which I could do already). He was grim
And full of bile at life. We hated him.
He held us in contempt. And that was that.

Said Scobie with his pole, *You'll swim from HERE*
To HERE. And I could do it easy-peasy.
Jimmy Buchanan, elbows, ears and knees,
Could not. *I'm frightened, Mr Scobie, please.*
He shrank from Scobie's apoplectic jeers:

Six months, boy, (prod) *and you can't swim ONE length?*
You need (prod) *backbone* (prod) *and discipline.*
The invertebrate screamed as Scobie shoved him in,
And screamed as someone dragged him out again,
Gaped like a fish and screamed. *Gawd gimme strength!*

Said Scobie, and we laughed. It was not us
Ineptitude had made ridiculous.

Cash Nexus Far Away and Long Ago

My Granny lived with someone we called Nana,
In a Bruntsfield flat, just up from Holy Corner.
Mirrors, mahogany, a kitchen range, a geyser,
Black flat irons, big brass taps, a sink so deep
Nana bathed me in it once. I had to sleep

In an iron bed with stone hot-water bottles,
To the clucks of the clocks and the grunts of the pipes and
            the cackles
And the creaks and the sparks of the trams across the cobbles.
And the bagpipes of a Regimental Band
Or *Kate Dalrymple* played by Jimmy Shand

From Nana's wireless. Then Nana's voice:
Will you be taking cocoa, Mrs Boyes?
Then Granny saying cocoa would be nice.
Granny called her Alice. Alice was her name.
Though we children called her Nana, all the same

She wasn't really. She 'did' for Granny …
And that was why she was Alice. All the money
Belonged to Granny. Alice hadn't any.
And so she made the porridge and the toast
And laid the fires with *The Sunday Post*

And she wasn't really Nana. It was funny.

My Dead Grandads

My mother's name was Boyes. I had, perforce
A grandad, Mr Boyes — alive in some
Sublime collateral continuum.
In this existence he was dead of course,
Shrunk to that little framed palladium

Up on my Granny's crowded mantelpiece.
With his hard black bowler hat, his black moustache
And his fierce black eyes, he scorned to cut a dash
Standing foursquare, as sure as the police,
He seemed to mock his imminent decease,

As unselfconscious as he was self-made.
But, at my Gran's, a smaller, plainer frame
Circled a gentler Grandad, much to blame.
A quarter of a century in trade
And Mr Whitworth's business never paid:

Though he scribed our name onto a carving knife,
Stage doors and lime light stole away his life;
Ironmongering made a bald and brutal noise.
So he failed and faded, left his pretty wife
And son to ruin. Not so Mr Boyes:

Even death could not disturb his equipoise.

So Romantic

My caustic, one-eyed Gran was Elsie Cuthbe.
I liked her chocolate biscuits, ten bob notes,
Old Boots' detective stories, anecdotes
Of life around the Diamond Jubilee,
Of Mafeking, flowery hats and button-boots.

He wore a ribboned boater; he was Percy;
He said she was like a willow wand, was Elsie;
We were star-crossed lovers, John. Which was absurd—
Such Pooterish names, and surely not our word,
Not mine at somethingteen nor hers at eighty.

His mother made him promise not to marry
Before his sisters, John. They were in no hurry.
So Elsie married someone else, the one
She didn't love and had a little son,
(This was my father), and was widowed early.

She opened up a hat-shop which did poorly,
(The Crash, the Slump, the world turned arsy-versy)
Bills piling up, her future such a blank
She walked out with the big-shot from the Bank
And so became a bride. *It was a mercy*

And so romantic, John. For this was Percy.

All Creatures Great and Small

I hated Scouts, the shorts, the silly hats,
And Euan Elliott to the nth degree.
Euan was tall, big-nosed, veal-coloured. He
Said EFFIN all the time, and hated me,
One o' they effin useless effin twats.

A Marxian subtext there: I understood.
And this commissar of pinch and jab and kick
Couldn't squeeze a tear from *me.* He was a thick
And went to a thicks' school. He made me sick.
Peter Kemp was big as well, but he was good:

He was freckled. He was friendly. He was nice.
At the Summer Camp I used to lie awake
In bestial misery. For Peter's sake
I'd stick it out. Yet goodness is opaque:
In a cloud of exhortation and advice

Peter's earnest influence began to die
Till the accident, the camp-fire cooking pot
That seared and scarred a channel down his thigh,
And the pain that made big, freckled Peter cry,
And the Love that should assuage it and could not.

The Big School

It grows from one of Edinburgh's seven hills:
This pagan temple on its jutty shelf
Extends its railway-blackened verticals,
Severe and chaste as Pallas is herself.
Yet fluted pillars, sheer retaining walls,

Their sweet Euclidean geometry,
Charm the barbarian granite of the cliff
Into a kind of Scots urbanity,
Inviolate (there's no front door) as if
Cold classicism likes humanity

A little at arms length. And cold we are:
In winter (memory denominates
At least eleven months of winter there)
Not scarves, gloves, scalding pipes or spitting grates
Can purge the impatient crispness from the air.

Let Rectors bleat, through practised, public lips,
Of character and commonwealth, we know
Winning, of rugby games or scholarships,
Is solid pudding, and we make it so,
Elitist to our frozen fingertips.

This Is My Own, My Native Land

At school one Catholic and forty Jews
Were absent at Assembly, and I'd guess
English Episcopalians like me could choose
The same sectarian exclusiveness.
But never being one to nurse the bruise

Of difference, I sweated at my text:
Och aye, I could say, *Ye ken*, and, *Whit fer no?*
Perhaps that last was going a bit far. Next,
The review of Scottish History's horrorshow
Left certain ancient loyalties perplexed:

Was Good Queen Bess, the Hammer of the Armada,
A conniving, flinty-bosomed, red-haired bitch?
She was. And were Jacobites good or bad? Much harder:
Bonny Dundee killed Presbyterians, which
Was very bad, but Charlie's martial ardour

(Losing the scabbard), rightly understood,
Since Southern Epicenes are scarcely missed,
Made him a kind of Tartan Robin Hood.
Like the bluff, rugger-playing Nationalist
Kneeing my Sassenach balls in—that was good.

Victim

When Alexander Ross sat next to me
He put his hand on my adjacent knee,
And did a recce very gradually.
My first affair at school and I was flattered.
I fear the moral aspect scarcely mattered,

Though, since it was an English class—the subject
I liked to shine at—being a sexual object
Grew tedious, and curiously abject,
The more so since I didn't give a toss
For itchy-fingered Alexander Ross.

He had no intellect; he was not witty;
He cut no ice among the school *banditti*;
A prat at games; though reasonably pretty,
Suffered from intermittent halitosis:
Being Sandy Ross was not a bed of roses.

One knows quite well it never makes you blind,
And everybody has a dirty mind,
Nevertheless … yet I was not unkind,
Nor even present when, behind the gym,
Political correctness saw to him.

Small Latin and Less Greek

From its temple gates the High School overflowed
Into the houses next to Regent Road:
Pillars and pediments and black lead grates,
The Consulate of the United States,
Superior old properties, and it showed.

Dark suits and waistcoats taught the Classics here;
The little boys would piss themselves with fear
As upright, stern, reactionary men,
Cut to an older fashion even then,
Bore out the language bristly on the bier.

TIBERIUS could poke the index finger
On his left hand straight through an apple or
A small boy's skull. He had no reverence
For the gods and thought the world was ruled by Chance.
He was deeply read in ancient literature.

IAN CHARLESON, who played Hamlet at the National
And died too young, drank Asti in a brothel
Near the Colosseum (he said). At Pompeii
I smoked sour local fags with GEORGE McDOUGALL
Who joined the Edinburgh C.I.D.

Musis Respublica Floret
It says on my old school prefect's badge. You bet.

Mad Aboot Fitba'

Stench of the changing rooms—I wish I'd stood
Outside their crapulous conspiracy,
The hoggish, red-eye, jock-strap brotherhood
Steaming in comfortable brutality.
The sad truth is I wasn't any good;

Yet the whistle shrilled and I hustled to their call.
Could bubblegum-card stars be made not born?
In priestlike solitude I'd coax a ball
As it sliced, ballooned, grubbed, trickled down the lawn.
Sometimes it didn't bloody shift at all.

If, at my Edinburgh secondary school.
Pretension substituted an ellipse
And hands as well as feet, it was just as dull
But dangerous too, with slaps, pokes, jabs, knees, trips,
Hacks, bites, to make me doubly miserable

With my fathomless ineptitudes revealed
And Saturdays swishing by. How is it then,
When the hard, white thighs of Scotland scorn to yield,
Humbling beef-faced and arrogant Englishmen,
My misrememberings wrap me like a shield

As Bannockburn resumes at Murrayfield?

A Word on Bullying

The English are good folk to go among;
Tractile, unused to violence of the tongue,
Their natural aggression is inchoate:
But Scots are hard, hard men. A Scottish poet
Is still a hard, hard man and lets you know it.

Be nice to people; they'll be nice to you —
My English lesson but it isn't true.
Better to learn the butcher-bird, the Shrike
That sticks his enemies up on a spike,
Better to learn pre-emptive counterstrike

And love your enemies as I love mine:
I treasure him, my own, my Valentine,
Valentine Tudball—this exultant Jock
With the amazing handle, thought to mock
My name, and turn me to a laughing-stock.

Why did he? Why? You snivelling hypocrite,
Because he *could*. Eh Whitworth? Worth a wit?
Eh Shitworth? Worth shit all? Bang on, sweet slanger,
My handsome Valentine, my bold haranguer,
My stormtroop darling and my doppel-ganger.

My Short and Glorious Career as a Tart

It was fixed by phone: an urgent voice would say
Are you SEXUALLY inclined? (he talked that way).
If so (it was always so) he'd come to tea
And in twenty minutes he'd be doing me
And I'd be doing him. This was OK

This was the stuff those foreign doctors meant
By EARLY PUBERTAL EXPERIMENT
(We were both of us thirteen); it did not show
Any propensity to be ... well—bent.
Relevant literature had told me so;

Propped up on scuffed, elastoplasted knees
Down unfrequented aisles of libraries,
It reassured me I was QUITE ALL RIGHT
And did not have the Oscar Wilde disease.
I couldn't speak for him of course—*he* might.

The plughole sucked. Re-editing my text,
I found I shouldn't be at all surprised.
I combed, I talcumed, I deodorised.
I kissed the bathroom mirror. *Oversexed*
And he wants me FOR MY BODY, I surmised

Wildly, deliciously, and shut my eyes:
I'd play it cooler when he came round next.

The Burning Bush

We were doing something after school (I can't
Remember what), and, when we'd done, we went
For a swim, no towels or trunks. And, in a way,
(Though of course I wasn't daft enough to say)
It was a personal Liberation Day.

I changed in frantic silence, double quick;
I was ashamed to show my peasant prick;
I hated it, and in particular
The fairy ring of crinkled reddish hair
Onset of puberty had rooted there

I hated (once, supposing they would scoff,
With soap and razor blade I shaved it off —
Futile of course), so dived into the pool
Before some ivory-skinned, unblemished fool
Remarked the foliation of my tool,

And, surfacing, surprised a god—on fire,
Curling and crackling, glittering like wire,
From armpit, chest and belly, down to groin,
The colour of a freshly minted coin,
Barbaric, gorgeous and just like mine …

It'll freeze your bollocks off! He grinned at me
And I grinned back in male equality.

Sin City

My bum pal friend had built a radio.
(Sex wasn't all he did though he was hot.)
We both made aeroplanes and we would go
And fly them on The Links. Mine crashed a lot—
I was clumsy with my hands as he was not.

His wireless with its headphones and its crystal
(You called a radio a wireless),
His periscope, his bunk-bed and his pistol—
Air-pistol, sure, but pistol nonetheless—
Possessions that I wanted to possess,

His prissy way of talking and his paleness,
His relegation to the class below,
His private challenge to my public maleness
(He was a pansy—people in the know
Had whispered it was obviously so):

My Envy, Avarice and Pride were stronger
Than flickering Lust. We didn't telephone.
His bicycle stood at the gate no longer.
I flew my kamikaze planes alone
And Dad bought me a wireless of my own.

Wordsearch

The CURSE has come upon her. Over there!
And I drop my Latin Grammar book to stare
And I laugh (it's safe to laugh). How does he know?
And why don't I? And is it really so?
I see a brightness falling from the air

And I'm desolate for being dirty-minded,
Spelling all words S-E-X the way his kind did:
BALLS in Jane Austen, BREASTS in Shakespeare, rude
Bits biroed onto every Art Room nude.
If there *is* a double-meaning, then I'll find it.

Money can't buy the word I *want* to say,
Though The Beatles haven't said it yet — OK?
Sweet, true, everlasting, many-splendoured, simple,
It will walk right in as sudden as a pimple,
It will change your lonely life one lovely day.

Poets write about it. Over mugs of tea
Women natter on about it endlessly,
Like my sister with her friend. We're very pally:
Could I ask her to the ballet? She likes ballet.
I wonder what she thinks of poetry.

I wonder what she thinks of me. Of me.

Love

Not first. I'd kissed my blue-eyed Gillian by
The swings (I was six), but this was not the same.
Now, pores awash with sex and sebum, I
Knew Love was serious business, not a game:
Vertiginous, evasive, full of blame,

My Love was lasting pain and sudden joy,
My Love was stained glass windows, incense, candles,
My Love was ashes of a second Troy,
My Love was woollen socks and light-brown sandals,
My Love was twelve years old, a little boy

Called Lindsay Patterson, with straight red hair,
A little boy, a little BOY! How could
God *do* a thing like that? The neighbourhood
Was stiff with GIRLS. It wasn't any good,
A holocaust of love I couldn't share

With anyone. When my friend Colin fell
In love, he wrote her name onto his jotter
In seven different biros just to tell
The French class and the world at large he'd got her—
I suffered Love in silence. Bloody hell.

Everything is Permitted

THE WORST DAY OF MY LIFE. MUM DIED. But when
The Infirmary doctors gave us something else
That wasn't death, it was back to God again.
I'd read George Bernard Shaw and H.G. Wells
And thought I'd stopped believing in Him then,

But No—I was on my knees beside my bed
Bargaining. *I'll be good.* It was not enough.
I'll believe in You. Pshaw! *You could take Dad instead.*
Or anyone. Now that was talking tough.
My neck-hair bristled. God was in my head.

He raised an eyebrow, stroked His Shavian beard
And grinned. All those years of nightly Bible-study
And I treat Him like some kind of Druid's Weird
Who must have blood to stop Him acting bloody.
Do I think the Future can be engineered

For my convenience? That He'd collapse
The Universe for me and mine? That Heaven
And Hell can be turned on and off like taps?
Do I believe in Magic, Lucky Seven,
It's-In-The-Stars and Rabbits' Feet perhaps?

Your mother dies. God dies. You've made a start
On Sex, and Politics, and sodding Art.

Getting to Go

When we'd done with Sunday school, she wasn't there.
Not then. Not soon. Not ever. No more Mum.
She had fallen on the landing by the stair,
Just coming up, and now she would never come.
Though I prayed and cried and prayed, God didn't care.

In The Edinburgh Infirmary she lay
On life support. We did not get to go,
And how she looked at last I cannot say.
They told us all they thought we ought to know.
My father went to see her every day,

Bess who had laughed and talked and smoked as late as
Twenty past two on Sunday afternoon,
Now emptied into absence, a hiatus
As uninhabitable as the Moon,
Something connected up to apparatus.

He watched the picture of Elizabeth
Jean Boyes, who was fat and witty, who was good
And kind and lost her temper, watched her breath
Pumped in, sucked out, her tubes, her bottled blood.
He watched the whole technology of death.

All this I think. Of course I do not know.
We did not see. We did not get to go.